STEP BY STEP GUIDE TO SELF PUBLISHING NOTEBOOKS AND LOW CONTENT BOOKS ON AMAZON

Written by CAH Productions

I0504495

Disclaimer

Introduction

First of all, let me thank you for making an investment in me and also yourself by purchasing this book. This method of making passive income online is certainly one of the most exciting and fun methods I have ever done. If you are a creative person, then you will simply love it. Actually, you may even learn to love it if you are not so creative. Let me start off by saying this is in no way a get rich quick scheme as many profess it to be. No, this is like any other business model; you must add value and stand above the competition to get results. More is more sometimes. Throughout this book, we will go through everything step by step and have your first book published ASAP. This is a no BS guide. I hate buying a product that says you will make $10,000 in a month or $100 overnight after reading it. Going off-topic a bit here, let me be the bearer of bad news, these are modern-day snake oil salesmen or women and the only one to get rich is the seller, which is why I have written this book. I want to show you the easiest way to publish no content books that will stand up to the test of time, while all the spammers get their accounts barred or terminated. We will focus primarily on notebooks for the method section of this book, as this has certainly made up 70% of my sales. Right off the bat, I had 78 books listed before I made a single sale, and many others were even higher. This is normal. Mind you, I didn't have a guide to help me and I made many mistakes, but now that you have this guide, let's try and get you sales faster. At the end of this book, I will share some of the resources I used that have helped me massively. Let's get started.

What are LCBs?

Low content books are books designed for a certain type of person, with minimum or no writing. For example, notebooks for whale lovers. They are really easy to make but take some time to get used to the designing and listing process. LCBs are a great opportunity right now for the entrepreneur who loves to make income online and is looking for a simple side hustle or potential full-time job whilst also loving getting artistic and creative. Be warned, passive income doesn't mean list one book and make $100 the day after, this will take time and I cannot emphasise this enough. LCB is not a scam that promises you lots of easy money immediately, so if you see these kinds of adverts, click away. LCBs will take time to create, market and list, but you can get a good library of books listed and reap the benefits almost immediately.

You need no special skills to start this adventure, but you must be willing to learn and take note of what works and what doesn't work. You may not be a great designer now, but when Muhammad Ali was born, he was not at all a good boxer, let alone the world's greatest, so keep learning and take the steps in this book first, then better them. You should always aim to better your sources in business, many self-proclaimed influencers are cringing at the thought of been outdone, but I personally want you to sell better than me... this is not a race, bear that in mind.

Advantages of LCBs

Low content books or LCBs are easily the best way to start a business as a new entrepreneur. They require no storage or manufacturing on your part, have virtually no overheads, and can be scaled in your own time. The best thing for me is that they require no customer services. This has crippled me before and really drained me of energy, especially when customers complain. Amazon takes care of everything from simply making the quality product and listing it, but you should also consider marketing if your book is doing well.

You will need:

Before you start your business, you will need a computer or laptop, this will be the heart of the operation. I'm going to assume you have one already, but if not, you may want to finance one. I strongly discourage debt, but if you work every day and stick to this method, over time, you will make your money back. Another option is to share one with a family member, you can even offer to pay them if they need tempting. Next up, you will need a reliable internet connection; this business model involves a lot of design elements that are utilised through a programme called Canva, so you will need an internet connection for every single aspect of this new venture. The next physical thing you need is a strong will to not give up, this is self-explanatory, but I have been doing low content for a little over a year now, and I have seen people come and go overnight. Most people won't see substantial growth for 6 months, the exceptions are either what are called unicorns (very rare) or liars (far to common). I remember in a Facebook group one guy was boasting about how his book he listed a day ago was crushing it, then it said in the top right that it was listed in 2017... what a dork. This concludes the physical things you will need. Now, you will need some software, and the good news is that they are all free. Canva is a simple design software, although I use the paid version now. You can start with the free version and reinvest your profits if you wish. I strongly recommend doing this as often as possible, Canva will be used for designing the book cover and the book interior. Others use Microsoft programmes, but I do it all in Canva. Simply visit www.canva.com and sign up for a free account. Next, you will need a Google Slides account, which is where you will put your interiors together. This sounds complex, but trust me, I'm as thick as 2 planks so you'll catch on quickly. Simply head over to www.google.com/slides and follow the instructions. If you are struggling with an email address, create a new Gmail account for free.

Next you will then need your KDP or Kindle Direct Publishing account, so head over to www.kdp.amazon.com and click sign up. If you already have an Amazon account, you will be able to log into it with that, but if not, you will have to create one, so go to Amazon.com or .co.uk, or whichever domain region you are in. On KDP, you will have to fill out a few details, including payment details, so have this information at hand, you may also need your tax code or national insurance number (UK only) to get paid. Don't overthink this step and don't procrastinate like I did, get your account set up and you will be one step closer to making some money online. One last thing on Kindle Direct Publishing, they pay out your royalties monthly but it can take up to 3 months to get your first royalties, this is a security feature for Amazon and it is what it is. You can't really do anything about it. Other software you will need to install are a few Chrome extensions, and Chrome itself. If you don't already have Chrome, log on to www.google.com/chrome and install it. Now, you should be able to download your Chrome extensions. The first one is DS Amazon Quick View, which will save you time by not having to click into every listing when you are researching. Simply search on Google for this and add it to your toolbar. Keywords Everywhere is your next tool and, again, this will help with your research, but this time, it helps research keywords. Finally, you will want to install AMZ Suggestion Expander, which will expand Amazon's recommended searches and give you more keyword options too. Now, to install these, either visit the Chrome store or do a quick search on the web bar. After installing them, they will appear at the top right side of your toolbar. They are all free and should definitely be utilised. Understandably, this is a lot to take in and you may want to just spend some time setting your device up for this, so take that time and don't rush it. When all of your accounts are sorted out, you will need one last thing. Time. Many people treat this as a side hustle, others as a full-on business, ultimately, this is up to you. Just put the work in daily. At first, I was doing 3 hours a day and reading and watching YouTube videos like a hawk, learning, trying to figure out Amazon marketing and such, so always dedicate some time for learning and work on your venture daily. One thing that I find helps me is having a relaxing place to work every night, so if you can get into a quiet place and put some music on in the background, you will be amazed at what you can get done.

The chrome extensions

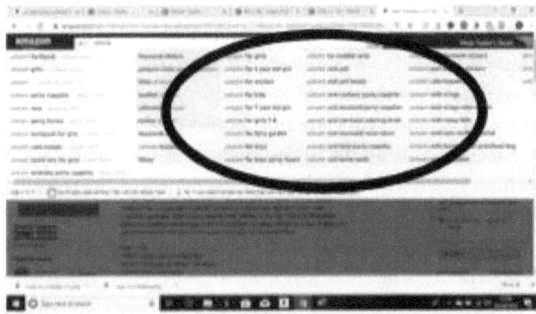

AMZ suggestion expander will give you a much bigger list of results to work with, this is great for getting keywords.

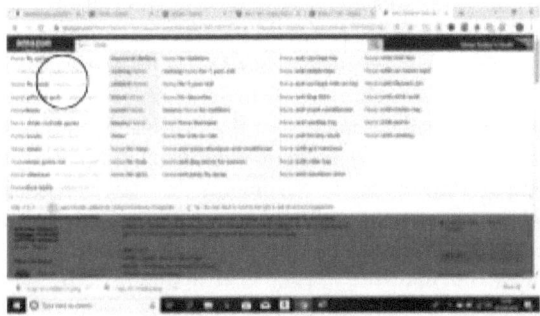

Keywords Everywhere tells you the monthly searches on Google for that particular keyword. This is great for judging if a keyword is relevant or not, as more searches mean a higher chance of selling.

Do not include FBA sellers in your research.

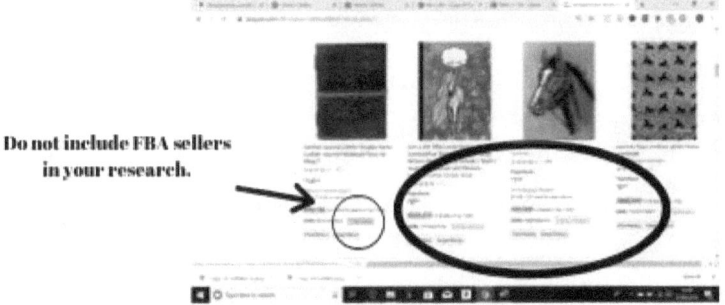

DS Amazon Quick View lets you see BSRs and other information without clicking into the product listing, this will save you time with your research.

Niche selection

Now you are totally set and ready to go. As promised, I'm not going to bombard you with pointless information. So, let's get into it. The first thing you must do is select a niche to cater to. Many self-proclaimed gurus suggest publishing 10-20 books in 2 niches a day, but this will lead to a complete burnout on your part and Amazon, who are a customer-based marketplace, will eventually clamp down on it. So, instead, still aim for 2 niches a day, but aim your notebooks towards a certain demographic and go for no more than 4 notebooks in 2 niches, or better still, 2 high-quality notebooks in 2 niches. You need to really find ways to add value and make your notebooks stand out, I will show you how to do this in a later chapter. Firstly, you must come up with a good list of niches to select. A niche is basically a topic or hobby... anything can be a niche, for example, hockey, football, fishing, etc. are all niches, these are broader niches as they focus on a certain topic, but you can niche these down further, for example, fishing> Sea Fishing > Sea fishing lures. It is always a good idea to think of something you know about first, for me, it was boxing, then niche it down to make sense, for example, Boxing> Boxing Workout> Skipping rope. There really are unlimited niches to publish in, but you must first determine if a niche is worth your time and has proven sales. The other thing to take into consideration is evergreen or seasonal niches. I recently sold around 107 copies of a schoolbook as it was the end of the summer holidays, this is a seasonal niche as people wanted back to school equipment for their children, therefore, there was a massive influx in demand. You can do this around any holiday really if demand is there, be it Christmas, Halloween or even holidays in other countries if people will buy them. The other type of niche is evergreen, which basically means year-round sales. This can be hobbies, for example, but you won't typically get as much success. However, that should not dissuade you and instead should excite you to tackle these niches and aim for consistent sales, or at least as near to consistent as you can get. I tend to play around with both. Two months before a seasonal holiday, I will publish notebooks and let them marinate. Note that not all books will sell. Some will sell way better than others, and we will go into detail on this later.

MY METHOD

Here, I reveal my method for listing notebooks on Amazon. The process is the same for any type of low content book. I like to see that a niche is selling well first rather than guessing the market. Let's start with selecting a niche and end with hitting publish.

How to find a niche

To find a niche, you must first build a sellers list. This is a common tactic in the drop shipping world and basically means finding sellers doing the same as you, that way, you can find niches they are publishing in and add it to a spreadsheet of niches. To make a sellers list, you will need a spreadsheet, which you can do on Google Sheets, then log onto Amazon.com and enter any keyword you can think of such as 'Goldfish Notebook', this is an example and if you are struggling to think of a niche keyword, think of your hobbies or things your friends do, etc. Now you will have a few books in front of you, so go through them and look at which ones you think you could create a better, more appealing cover. At this point, you are hunting for authors who publish rubbish looking notebooks. When you find something, click on the author name, here you will see in the top left how many books they have listed. Have a quick scroll through and see how many of their books are selling and also see if they have a higher number of books, the number of books is less important if their books are selling well, but you will have more niches to choose. Be sure to note any best seller rank that are lower numbers as the lower the number, the higher the sales. If you find a seller that is selling no books, you can discard that seller, but you may want to do a quick search on Amazon if the niche sounds like something you have never heard before. Aim to create a list of 100 sellers, this will take some time, but will prepare you for having an easier selection process.

Finding a seller for your seller list.

Enter your source keyword. In this case, 'goldfish notebook' in the Amazon search bar
and click the search button.

Author names are
here, but I've had to
blank these out for
privacy reasons.

Scroll down the list and find a simple design that you think you could make look better and
click on the listing. When inside the listing, click on the author's name (pen name).

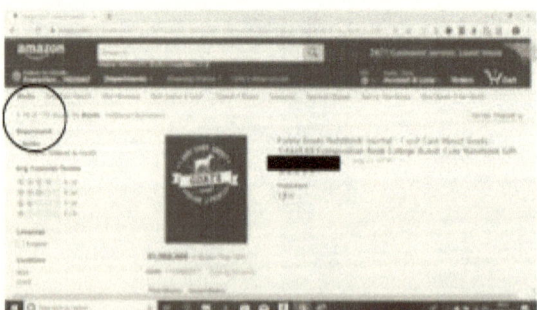

Note how many results they have, this is the number of books in their library under this
pen name, copy the link and add it to a spreadsheet.

How to know if a niche is good

Now you have a solid sellers list, you can start selecting niches to publish in, so on your sellers list spreadsheet, click on your first seller and scroll through their books until you find a niche that is selling well. To determine if a book is selling well requires a few steps. The first thing you should look for is the best seller rank, or BSR, which is a number with a # before it that tells you how good or bad a book is selling. A BSR of #1000000 or higher is not doing well but may sell a copy per month at best. A BSR of #24000 is likely selling a copy per day or more. This is a vague analytic and you will find over time that the BSRs can change as often as every hour. In my opinion, aim for a BSR of #900000 or less. The lower the number, the higher the demand, but this still doesn't guarantee sales. Let's say you find a niche that is #300000, that is not a bad number and has the potential to sell a few copies a month, so take the niche keyword and type it into Amazon, followed by 'notebook' or 'journal'. For example, 'parrot notebook' or 'parrot journal'. Next, you must note the number in the top left corner that says 'results', which is how much competition you have. Then click the categories button on the Amazon search bar and click 'books'. I tend to see the number drop dramatically here. As you are publishing on KDP, you will instantly be placed in 'books', so try and do all your research in the books category on Amazon as it is easier and more accurate, but feel free to see what the wider competition is doing too, as they could be selling stuff like mugs and t-shirts but have 'book' as a keyword, which is poor practice... but that is not my place to judge. Now that you have a potential niche chosen with a BSR of #900000 or less, check the results number again and aim for less than 1,000 results. You can always start your niche searches in the books category, I just like to see what the results number is before and after. If it all matches up, scroll through the books and see the average BSR of the other books here, if there is only 1 with a good BSR but the others are average or bad, then there is demand, but not a lot, so I would discard it as the aim here is to get you sales and not wing it. If there are a few BSRs with good numbers, then you are on to a winner. Around 3 or more is a good estimate. Also, be wary of sponsored listings that display the sponsored label or products sold through the FBA programme, these will have a little red FBA box on the listing. The more research you do, the easier you will find it to win. Note all the niches down and keep going, I do all my niche research on a Sunday ready for the week, but there are people who do it every day. Find out what works best for you, choosing the correct niche is crucial for your success. If you are struggling, see the pictures for more help. Note that a BSR number is only shown when a book sells.

What makes a great niche.

Search category set to books.

Search result below 1000.

BSR below #900000.

You will find that not every seller on your sellers list is the same, these are the signs of a good niche in a practical situation.

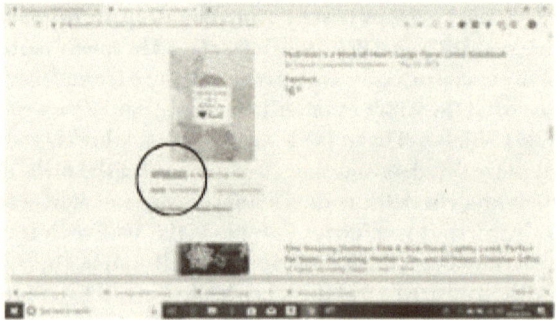

Scroll down the results page and try and find at least 3 listings under #900000, making sure they are sold by Amazon and not sponsored.

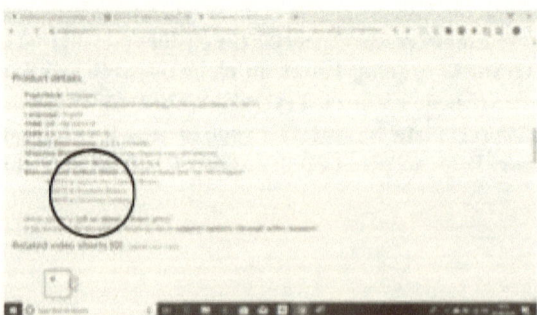

Take note of designs that sell well and categories that the book is selling in.

Making your product

Now you have a good list of niches that you want to publish in, you must build your notebook with your target customer in mind. Think age, gender, hobbies, thoughts and try and come up with a prospect avatar. This is who your customer should be, so if you are publishing a notebook for a car mechanic, pick a specific type of person, so a man or woman mechanic, pink cover or blue cover, gushy quote or serious quote on the cover, maybe an image. See what is selling on Amazon already to get a good understanding. Next, you must decide on the size. This is a highly debated and often overthought concept in low content book publishing, but the average size I see for notebooks and journals are 6 x 9 inches and 120 pages. You will have to ultimately decide this, but anything over 120 pages is too big in my opinion and the customer may complain that they cannot write near the spine of the book as it is too tight. KDP don't do ring binders and the books can be difficult to write in the middle. You will need 2 measurements here, one for the cover and one for the interior. I do all my interiors on Canva, where you can simply choose the trim size you want. Amazon let you publish in a lot of trim sizes, but I have rarely published outside of 6 x 9 inches. People tend to overthink this, but it has no or very little impact on your sales, in my opinion. If you feel you want to branch out, then I highly recommend Tangent Templates, I am not at all affiliated with them, but I strongly advise this software, it is a one-time payment and will give you exact dimension for every trim size, page number and more. For now, though, stick to 6 x 9 and 120 pages,

the dimensions for your full cover in Canva are:
6 x 9 inches with 120 pages: Full cover 12.52 in x 9.25 in
8.5 x 11 inches with 120 pages: Full cover 17.52 in x 11.25 in
7 x 10 inches with 120 pages: Full cover 14.52 in x 10.25 in

Stick to these for now, and bear in mind that this is for your exterior book cover. For your interior, use the exact measurement on Canva, like 6 x 9 inches. If you want to try a different size but can't afford the software, then you can work the measurements out by downloading a template from here: kdp.amazon.com/en_US/cover-templates, and then figure out the spine dimension. On the template, there will be a spine width, now you must add the cover together, so a 6 x 9 inch would be 6+6, then add the spine dimension which is 0.27 and then add the bleed which is .125, then add the bleed again which equals 12.52. Now you can see why I hate changing the interior dimensions so much, but with a bit of practice, you will get there. Here is what the dimension would look like: 6+6+0.27+0.125+0.125=12.52, the bleed is always the same and refers to the space around the outside.

Making the cover

So, after you have decided the trim size, load up Canva and hit 'create new design', then hit 'custom dimensions'. Make sure it is set to inches and type in whichever dimension you have chosen, which will then give you a blank design to be your cover. You now need a template, which you should have already downloaded from www.kdp.Amazon.com/en_US/cover-templates. After the template has downloaded, click 'upload' on Canva's left interface and when it has loaded, click on the template and expand it to fill the page. You will notice the red areas around the outside, this is where words cannot cross over, your book will be rejected at the review stage with Amazon if you have writing here. Now, think of the customer avatar you came up with earlier and, again, use other books in a niche as a template, but don't copy other people's work. You will eventually get banned if they complain to Amazon and it's just poor practice. There are many design options to go with, but I often find a good quote or fancy pattern with a quote specific to that niche will sell the best, so head over to pinterest.com and type in your niche name, followed by 'quote' for some great quote ideas. When you find a quote, you can redesign it in Canva. Just do a quick check to see if it is legal to use, I use Trademark Eagle for this. Below, I have shown a few examples of covers you could use, you will soon see what designs work well for you, but avoid the simpler ones. Less is more, but a blank background with 'get s*** done' on it is lazy and will not sell as well as a thought out cover. Think of your customer avatar and what colour/colours they would prefer, for example, a women's notebook could be pink/purple/green/red/blue. But for a man, you would want to steer clear of pink and purple and maybe opt for a red design. You can play with the text fonts and images or graphics (I cover these in more details below). Canva is good for newbies as you can use the drag and drop style of designing on Canva.

Full cover template on canva

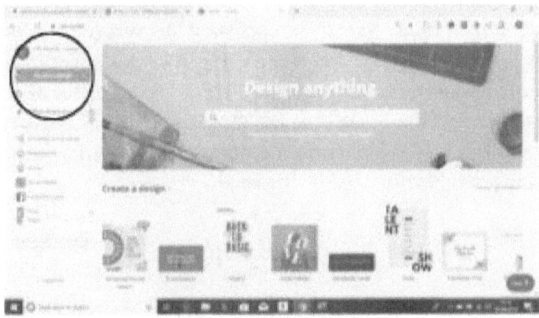

Log in to Canva and on the top left, click 'custom design' and make sure it is set to inches.

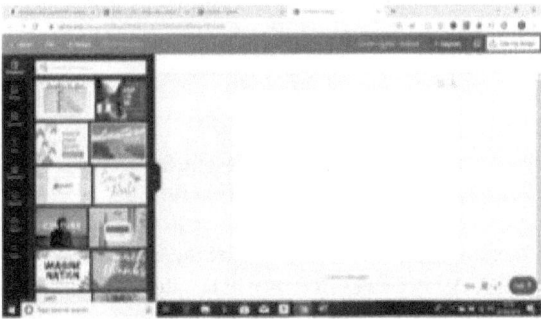

Print your dimensions in and you will have your design in front of you, just like this.

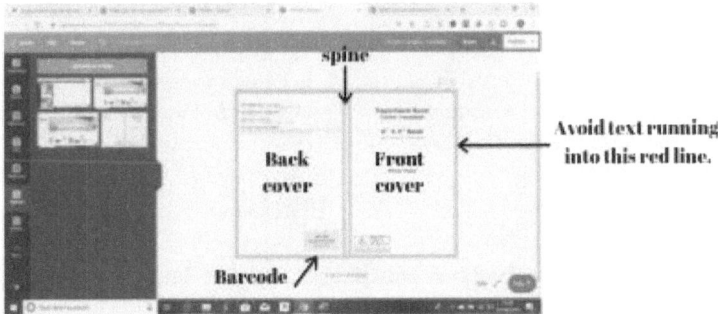

Extend the template you downloaded from Amazon and now you have a design template.

Elements

This is where you will find your shapes, graphics and more. You will spend a lot of time using these elements and you can either search through each section manually or do a search in the bar at the top for what you are looking for. Some elements may be copyrighted. To check if a certain graphic is copyrighted, click the little dots and look at the license, if it says 'free to use' on all of your designs, you are ok, but never just have one graphic on your design at once, try and make a collage or pattern. You will have all of your shapes here too, including lines which we will cover in the interior section of the book.

Photos

This is where you will find royalty-free images, but again, follow the steps above to see if they are free to use in your designs. Only in circumstances of making a notebook for people's careers will I use an image, but it is rare. If you're struggling to figure anything out, email Canva and they will help you out really fast.

Text

This is where you will create your wording design. By clicking 'text', you will be given a few options, the pre-made texts are great for finding word pairings for your quotes that are ready-made by professional designers, so note the pairings down but always make your own design by clicking 'add header' and do it manually. You will get a better result as it will be more personalised, and you can play around with fonts. Spend some time getting used to Canva's text feature, it is drag and drop, so easy to use.

Background

This will give you a drop-down of backgrounds, as ever, check to see if you have copyrights. I rarely use backgrounds because I prefer to search backgrounds in photos or elements or make my own patterns in Canva. An example would be marble or tartan effect.

Uploads

Here, you will upload your own images. This is a simple and useful feature to get your own designs or photos into Canva.

More

There are a few extras here, but for the most part, you won't need them.

Another resource for pictures is www.pixabay.com, these are royalty-free images, but right-click on the photo and search Google for the image, this will show you if the image has come from another website that wants royalties. If you see it on another site, don't use it. When you have an element or photo selected in Canva, you can sometimes change the colour on the top toolbar (far left) and also flip it, add a filter, adjust or crop, some of these options are not available in the free version though. It is the same principle with text, you can also duplicate and position. Again, get a feel for Canva, do some designs and take a day to familiarise yourself with the interface. Canva is designed for beginners, see the photos for clearer instructions if you are struggling. When you have designed a cover, hit the upload button in the top right and make sure it is saved as a PNG.

Canva's features.

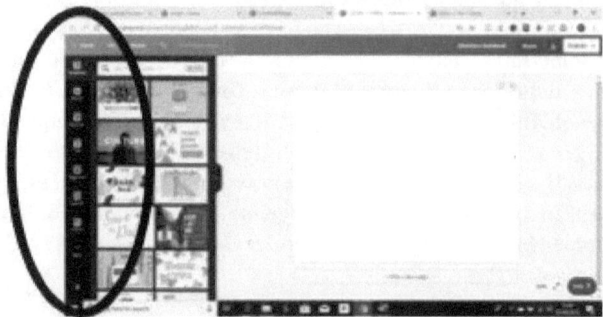

This is the taskbar where you will find all your design elements, texts, images and more. Take your time searching through this, you can either manually search through all the tabs or do a search in the tabs search bar.

When you select text, you will be greeted by this page, you can change the font, size, colour and more on the toolbar on the top left of the screen, everything is drag and drop.

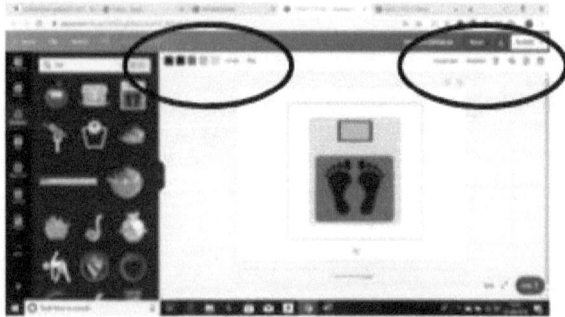

This is what you will see when you choose a graphic. Colour selection on the top left with the ability to crop or flip your image, and more options on the right, like transparency slider, position, great for moving layers forward or backwards and centre.

Examples of a good cover.

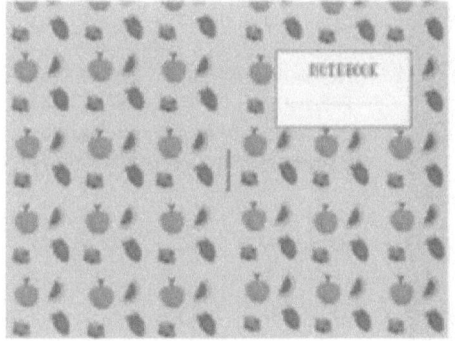

These simple pattern designs are a great option for a creative approach. Ultimately, it is up to you what to design, but a quick Google search of what colour schemes work will show you great pairings. Notice the book title is on the spine, you must have your title on the book somewhere.

Quotes on covers are a winner, just make them look nicer than your competition. You can do this by adding patterns and making your text really pop.

Images on notebooks are rare, but if done correctly, they can really resonate with your target audience. Here is an example of one, notice that it is a collage effect, I think they look a little better, so later I will show you how to list a notebook, and use this as an example.

Examples of a badcover.

There has been no thought put in here. A single graphic with the title on the spine is not the way to go, nobody will buy them anymore, not when the competition are uploading great designs.

Believe it or not, some influencers think this is all it takes to make money, but that is far from the truth, this product has no target market and took literally 40 seconds to put together, these designs are common on Amazon and the only useful thing is that the sellers have so many niches on their author pages that you can put in your sellers list.

These are actually live on Amazon right now, and these scalable designs simply cannot last long. Amazon are very strict on these practices and will eventually crackdown on them.

checking a copyright on Canva

When you find a graphic, photo or element you like, you must check its copyright. Do this by clicking the 3 little dots on the top right of the graphic.

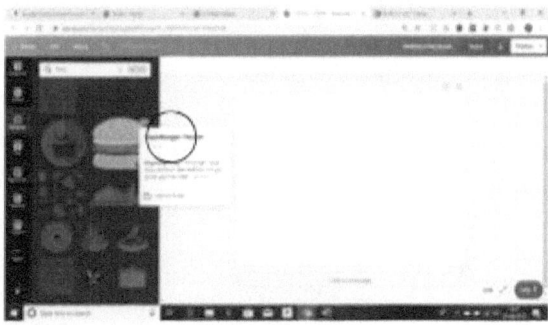

Click the three dots and then you must click the element's title.

You will be greeted with this page in a separate tab, and you want to see that it is free to use in all of your designs.

Interiors

Focusing on notebooks again, make another custom dimension for the size you have chosen. These interiors you make can be used over and over and are saved in Canva, although I would do something different to each of the interiors in some way. Now go to elements and search 'line', then shrink it down and make it black or dark grey (whichever you think looks best). Make sure the line isn't too thick or thin (see my example), now hit 'duplicate' until the lines are nearly at the bottom of the page, highlight them all and click 'position' then 'centre'. This will create your notebook lines. You can add smaller lines at the top to make diary-style books, but always keep the lines away from the edge, this is known as 'bleed' and your notebooks will be no-bleed. See my examples for this. Now, get creative and add an element that is specific to your niche and fade it to the background using the transparency feature. This will make your notebook stand out, you can even add a 'this book belongs to' page, which just adds value and gives your books more credibility. Again, I have done a few examples for you to use as a template. Save this as a PNG. Now you have made your product, it will take time and practice to get better. Avoid rubbish designs and product spamming, examples of these are on the previous pages. Now upload them from Canva and open Google Slides.

Interior template on canva

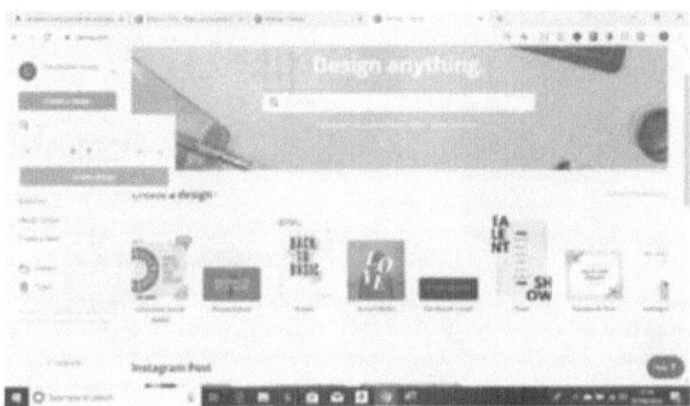

Add your dimensions into Canva for the interior and click 'create design'. Remember, your interior dimensions are the exact size of the trim you choose.

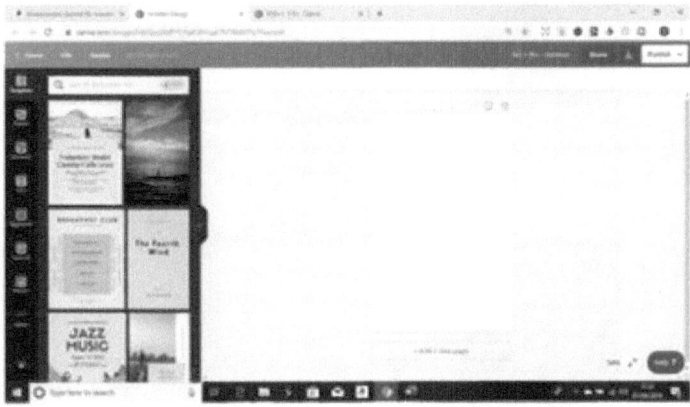

Now you have your interior template.

Interiors on Canva

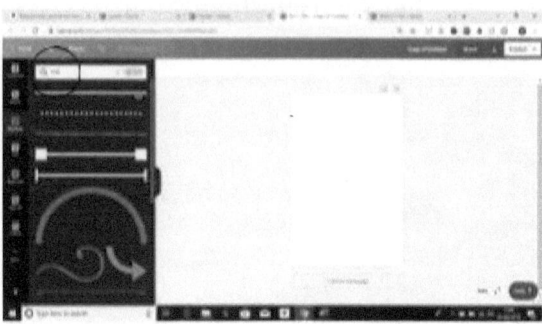

To make your interior, you can click the search bar in elements and search for 'line', select the line and drag and drop it into place, you can then make it smaller and make it black or grey. Then click duplicate until the lines disappear off the screen.

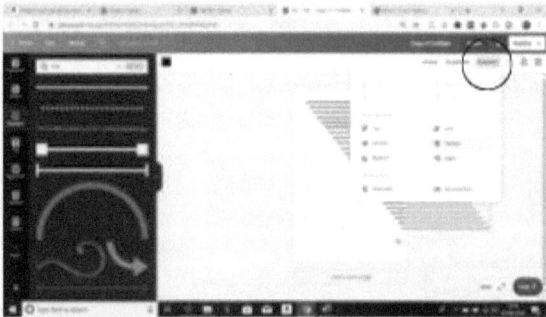

Now you have your lines, click 'position and centre', this will align your lines. You may want to add a few more lines and centre them all manually. This will give you a lined page to work with.

Get creative here, add an image or graphic, perhaps even a diary line at the top for title and dates. Be really creative as this may result in a good review on Amazon, which will really boost your product's visibility on the platform.

Add that value,

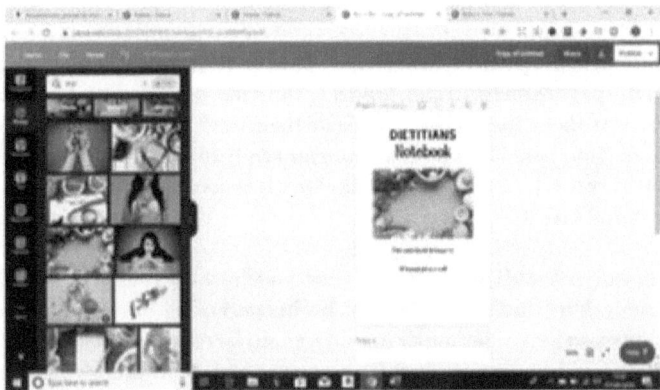

One great way to add something to your notebooks is to add a custom page before your lined pages, these are great for standing out. Don't be afraid to experiment.

These are examples of a notebook page you can do, when you do two different designs, they will look better in the book rather than just one design.

Putting the interior together

In Google Slides, click 'blank presentation' and go to file > page setup > custom and put in the dimensions of your book in inches. So, 6 x 9, for example. Click 'apply' and delete the text on screen, drag your design onto the pages and adjust it until you are happy, be aware of your bleed though, keep it away from edges. Now, on the left side of your screen, you can right-click on the page thumbnail and duplicate the slide, do this until you have a few and hit CTRL+C to copy them, then CTRL+V to paste them until you have the number of pages you have chosen. You should now have an interior ready to use. Simply click print or CRTL+P and where it says 'destination', make sure it is saved as a PDF. You can now check your document and save it.

That is the fun and easy stuff out of the way, now you must list your product on Amazon. This is easily done, but I find it to be the most boring part of the process, however, you may love it. Make sure you have some music on and remain focused. So, let's go through the steps you must take. First, log in to your KDP account and click 'publish paperback', here you will have to fill in your paperback details. I have gone into more detail below.

Title

The title must be on your book, either the front cover or the spine. Anything could be the book title and it will be indexed for keywords in order to help link customers to your book. To be honest, if it is a quote, use that or put the quote on the front and another title on the spine, this is simply done in Canva by making your writing size 9, turning it 90 degrees and clicking position then centre and middle. Keywords are words that link your buyer to your product, but these have their own section later.

Subtitle

This will not be on your book, but you want to use something that sells your book here and explains what it is. For example, 'hockey notebook for women', this is simple and sends a clear message, don't stuff keywords in as Amazon hates it and it looks awful. Again, these are indexed and will be active keywords.

Series

This is irrelevant to notebooks, but if you decide on doing low content books that serve a purpose, you may want to make a series.

Edition

Again, this is irrelevant to notebooks

Author name

This is where you will need a pen name. I have 3 different pen names, but don't use keywords here as Amazon may reject them. Use something that has a brandable feel to it and come up with a name, think of something unique to you, focus on one pen name first then add others as you go along. As ever, don't overthink this, but if you are struggling, you can always use your name. You're allowed as many pen names as you want, but only one KDP account, Amazon will ban you immediately for opening another KDP account, so bear that in mind.

Description

This is where you describe your book. Head over to www.kindlepreneur.com/amazon-book-description-generator/ for a free Amazon description. You really should do a description for each book that you publish and add a few keywords in here too, these are indexed in Google and will help customers find you from Google, but don't stuff keywords here, nobody will buy if your description reads 'notebook pink women's writing pad'. Think of your customer and tell them what problems your notebook will solve or why your notebook will make an excellent gift. Add bullet points at the end of your sales pitch. Feel free to use this as a template:

Niche (example hockey) is the greatest sport on the planet, perhaps you want to record a diary of all your team's successes. Well, this fantastic hockey-themed notebook is perfect for all of your writing needs, be it home, work or school use, designed to raise a smile on any hockey fan's face. Keep a diary or organise your lists in one beautifully designed place. This makes the most amazing hockey gift for the fan in your life. Scroll up and claim your copy today.

Notebook for all your daily needs
Blank lined pages to write in
Fantastic hockey-themed cover with quote
Great gift for hockey fan or player
6 x 9 inches, great for backpacks and bags
Finished with a dry wipe glossy effect

This description is only a guide, but it covers the basics. It starts by grabbing the reader's attention, not selling anything, it then highlights a problem they never knew they had, like needing somewhere to write, it then adds ideas such as keeping a diary, then includes a call to action by saying 'claim now'. The bullet points further enforce what the book offers and the keywords are not in your face and spammy. Get creative with your descriptions, sell the book, but don't be a robot saying this notebook is good and makes a good gift. Sell it, highlight its great points. In the description editor, you can make areas bolder that you want to pop out at the readers, so you should utilise this. Below is an example of a good description on a notebook
and then a bad one:

Description examples

So, firstly, this design is not good and the description is flat and boring, compare this to the design below and you can see why it is not selling.

The cover design for this book is fantastic and could be remade in Canva with different patterns, colours and quotes. The description is captivating if a little short, but lacks the bullet points. Most buyers will only look at bullet points as it is quicker.

Now we are talking, this description gives you solutions to problems that the customer never knew they had. It gives strong bullet points and emphasises what is great about the product. The design is basic but it sells well.

Keywords

I've mentioned keywords but not really explained them up to this point. Keywords are what your customer will type in to find your books, similar to what you do when researching. You will utilise the Chrome extensions here. AMZ Suggestion Expander will give you more suggested keywords when you type it into the Amazon search bar and Keywords Everywhere will show monthly searches, this is Google's information though as Amazon doesn't disclose this info, but it flows over onto Amazon too. There are 7 keyword slots and you are allowed 50 characters in each one, so try and utilise all the characters. You don't need to add the keyword 'book' into your keywords as it is already indexed and there are a few other words you should not use such as words you have in your title, subjective claims like 'best' or 'high-quality', and you can't use time-sensitive statements either, like 'available now' or 'on sale'. Also, avoid punctuation and definitely avoid trademarks like authors or movie stars, movies and sports teams as these are lawsuits waiting to happen. Actually, never make a notebook for trademarked products. You should ideally aim to get long tail keywords into your keyword areas as these are phrases that people are searching for. By using the Chrome extensions, you can find what people search for and create a list, start with a seed keyword like 'hockey journal' and see what else comes up. Another strategy is to type your seed keyword into the search bar on Amazon and note what other items come up like hockey, mask, gloves, mug, t-shirt, etc. then add these in after a long tail keyword, for example, hockey 'notebook journal for women gloves mug t-shirt'. See the examples below. Keywords are another crucial step, but ultimately, they won't sell the book like your design will. Continue your research on the subject as often as you can as strategies are forever changing and Amazon always update the rules. Note that you should only use a keyword once and try getting as many keywords in.

Keywords

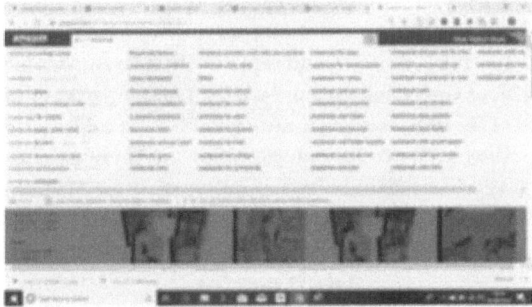

We can see here that by typing the word 'notebook' into the search bar has brought back many results, use keywords with higher searches that describe your book best.

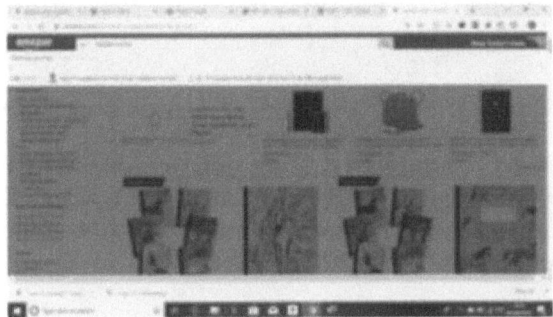

The word 'journal' is also a good option, although it should be made clear in your subtitle that it is a notebook. Search on other listings for keyword phrases you could use.

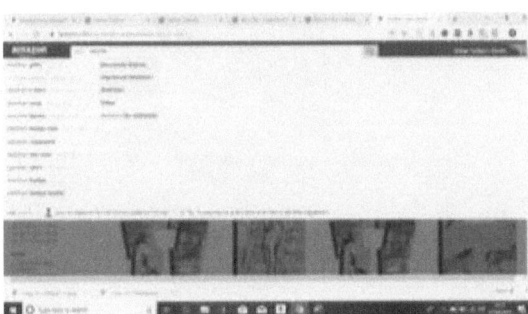

Here you can see what dietitians search for, use these after your long tail keywords as they can make impulse buys, again, only use the ones with higher search results.

Categories

Next up is the categories section. The categories are what link your books to the readers like a section in a library. The best course of action here is to see what categories your other readers are in and replicate it. Amazon has been known to move the categories of your books around without notice, so don't worry if they change at the end of the day. Amazon knows what they are doing, they do it every day. If a book is selling better in one category than another, use that category, but don't abuse categories like putting a hockey notebook in the travel category as it may have more visibility... Amazon will shut your account down fast.

Adult content

If you have no swearing or adult photos in your notebook, check 'no' then hit continue.

ISBN

This is a barcode that Amazon assigns to you, this actually costs Amazon money AND is why I suggest only 2-4 quality notebooks a day that you take your time with because Amazon will eventually get rid of the spammers that do 20-100 a day. Click 'assign me an ISBN', it's free and will be sorted out by Amazon. Note, if you are doing designs on the backs of your book (I rarely do), the ISBN will be a barcode in the bottom right of your design, templates have this on them.

Book options

Now you must select your trim options, starting with the page colour and design. Go for white paper with black and white ink, as this is much cheaper to print and gives you more profit. The cream paper is also a little thicker and will mess up your dimensions. Next up is the trim size, which will always start as 6 x 9 inches, so change it accordingly, then you have bleed or no bleed. Since you have space around the edge of your page, click 'no bleed', now choose between matte and gloss effect, this has no impact on sales as nobody really reads it, so go with whatever you feel is right. I usually choose the glossy effect. Now you can upload your interior manuscript that you made earlier.

Upload your cover and click the design that shows your book as it should look as if it is laid on a table (second design), delete all the text on the screen and hit 'preview', then if you are pleased with your preview, select 'continue and save'. This step may take a little while, so it will be the perfect time to grab a coffee. I tend to fill out all the metadata and have all four of my designs ready to go together in different tabs and do them in one go because it is much quicker. Tangent Templates has a listing helper which is a Godsend for this sort of stuff, but again, if you can't afford it yet, buy it when you can. I promise it is worth its weight in gold.

After your book has previewed, it should say all ok, but if it is red, you will have to locate the problem and fix it. This is usually when your interior is over the margins and can easily be rectified in Google Slides by making your lined page smaller. Now, you must price the book. Typically, people price their notebooks between $4.99 and $7.99, but don't price yourself out of the market. I recommend $5.99 or higher as the quality will show in your designs. Never be afraid of the competition who think they will get rich overnight by offering bargain bin prices, it just makes their products look cheap. Next, you should check the 'expanded distribution' box, this will give you further coverage as third party sellers will sell your books too, but be warned, you will get less royalty per sale. Go through all the regions and set a price, when you are happy, hit publish and you are done. You have published a book! Over time, you will get better with practice and by noticing patterns. If a book is selling well, create another book in that niche with a different design, this will scale your business.

Amazon takes up to 72 hours to manually check your books, so you must be patient in this time as they do it all by hand and, at busier times, they struggle to keep up. When your book is live, you will see an email from KDP saying it is live or that there is a problem, most problems are easy fixes, let's check them out.

Your title doesn't match the metadata - simply redesign or readjust the title. It is useful to keep your design in Canva until it is live, then you can redesign over it. I basically have 10 6 x 9 designs in Canva that are notebooks, and when I list one and it is live, I start on the other. Your title is too big for the spine - this usually means your title on the spine is too big, simply make it smaller in Canva. Author name is not accepted - you must have a keyword in your pen name that Amazon does not like, you can change this on your setup page.

List your book on KDP

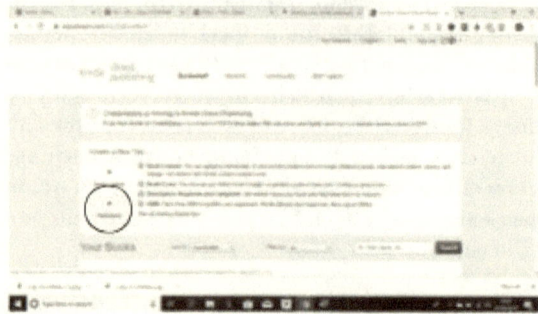

Firstly, log on to your KDP account and select paperback

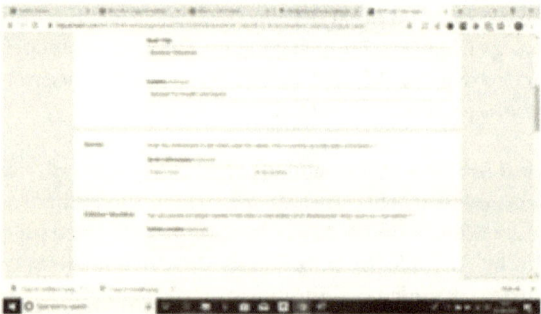

Now fill out your paperback details above. Some people have all the metadata ready in a notepad app on their device, but I use software for more leverage.

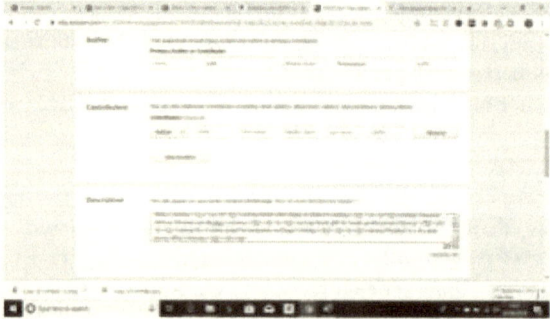

Continue filling out the first page, when using the description editor, you will have to copy it from the description creator tool and paste it onto the box, this will show you all the coding, saving you so much time as you do not have to learn it.

List your book on KDP

Do your keywords and choose your categories, simply look at others that are selling well. If you cannot find the category you want, email KDP and they will place it in that category. Select 'no adult content' and click 'continue'.

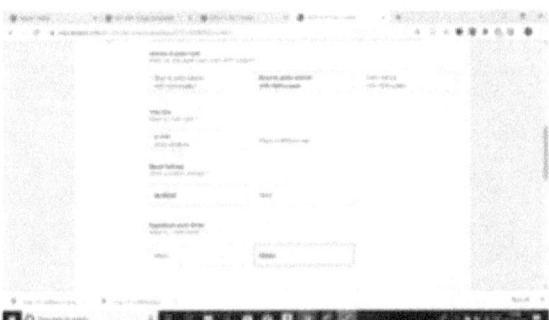

Assign an ISBN and scroll down.

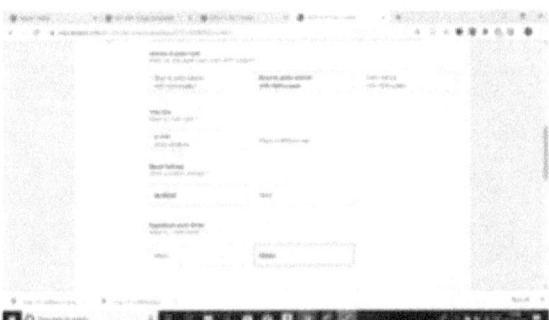

This is how I have all of my notebooks set up.

List your book on KDP

This is the screen that loads when you click 'upload cover', simply select 'upload from computer'.

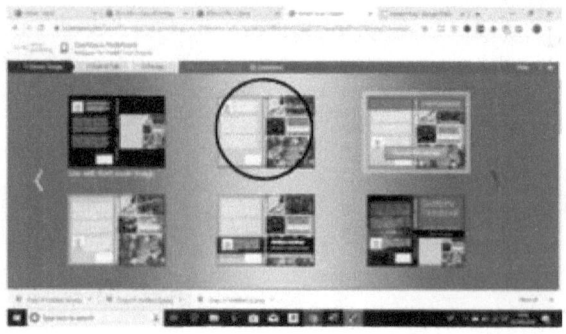

Now choose the middle design on the top row.

Delete all the on-screen text as it will show on your design if you do not, then hit 'preview'.

List your book on KDP

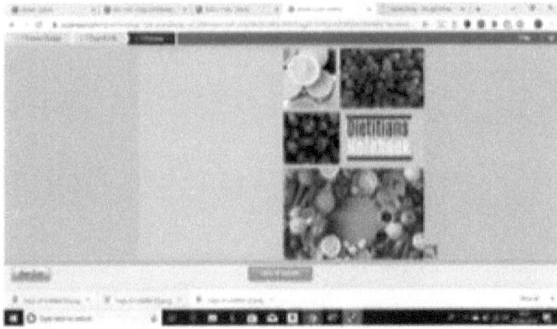

If you are pleased with the result, save and continue.

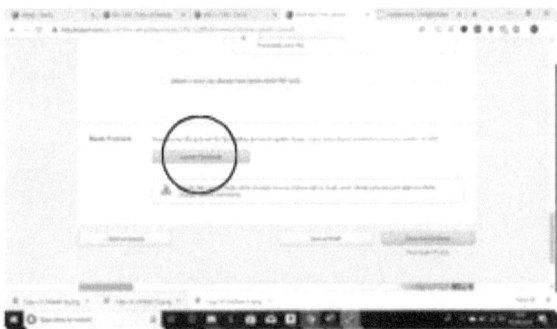

Now click 'launch previewer', this may take a while, but if after 20 minutes you are not done, restart the process.

When your product has had a quick check through with the Amazon software, you can go through it manually. If there is an error, it will say 'error' instead of 'please check'. If you are happy, click 'approve' and then save and continue.

List your book on KDP

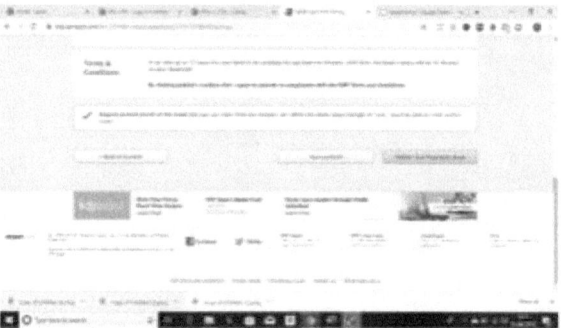

Now you must price your book, tick the expanded distribution box and go through all the marketplace.

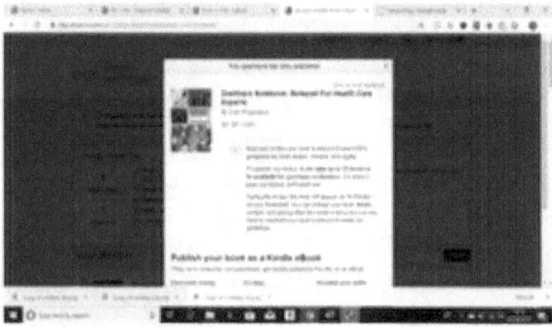

Finally, click 'publish your paperback'. You are now done. It is that easy.

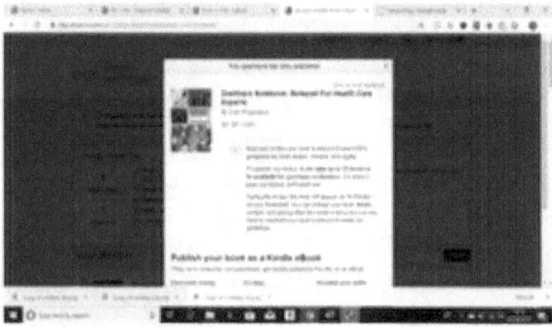

This is the last screen after you have published and you will see a little graphic of what your book will look like in the store. Now Amazon will manually check your book which may take several days.

Getting paid

If you have set up your payment details, you will automatically get paid into your bank account and will receive an email from each Amazon marketplace that you sold books in as each marketplace tracks things separately. You will also not receive your first royalties for 2-3 months as this is just Amazon policy, then you will be paid monthly. To check your results, log on to KDP and click 'reports', from here you can see how many books have sold, although you can only see book numbers that have sold here. To see the titles of the books that sold, click on 'month to date', then click on 'paperbacks'. If you see a red line, that is a distribution copy that has sold. Sales only show up when the notebook has been shipped to your customer, so be patient. In the beginning, avoid checking your results too often as this may dishearten you when you are getting going. You can also find out payment details in the report tab, so it is worth getting to know this section of your KDP back office.

Different types of LCBs

Now you know my strategy, you must learn about the other parts of this business model. We started on notebooks, but there are so many types of books you can publish, let's look at some:

Notebooks/notepads

I'm sure you are familiar with these by now, these are blank lined books that are specific to a certain person. You can add value by making the cover art better than your competition, also customise the insides a little bit to stand out. These are sometimes called journals.

Diaries, planners, organisers

These types of LCB are perfect for business people or workers on a tight schedule. Usually, they contain a calendar of some sort and at the very least a template inside to write on. You can get really creative with the interiors. By using the 'look inside' feature on Amazon (only available on desktop versions), you can see what the competition is doing, always aim to make your interior better as over time the rubbish will sink and the cream always rises.

Travel journals

These are my second favourite type of book to design as I am, by nature, a very adventurous person. A travel journal lets your customer record data from their trips like travelling or camping, etc. There are loads of options you can utilise here, again, check the competition out and maybe add some travel quotes to the interior. Never be afraid to experiment, you will always get better results if you are willing to take a risk and try something new. As with any of these books, a good sellers list will help you find niches.

Stress journals

These journals are basically designed to be abused, they let the user rip, tear, paint and pretty much anything else. They are fairly new concept and certainly have some potential, but as ever, do some research and take your time making these.

Prayer journal

These journals are obviously for religious people and can feature prompt questions, quotes and the like. They help people remember to pray and record daily religious activities.

Gratitude journal

These journals are used for people who practice daily gratitude, prompt questions, quotes, graphics, etc. Get creative and see what you end up with.

Colouring books

With certain software or a little education, you can create colouring books, they can be great for kids, adults and elderly people alike, they are niche-specific books and will be a great tool in your arsenal.

Puzzle books

These can include simple crosswords, Sudoku, etc. Again, you can use software to create the puzzles or do them yourself in Canva, but that is very time-consuming and I would recommend getting some software. Again, do all the interiors in Canva, it is so easy and follow the steps to make it into a journal on Google Slides too. Focus on notebooks at first though. These cover the basic low content books you can do.

You can also do sketchbooks, but be warned, Amazon does not allow blank pages, so you
will need something on each page, the same can be said for gag books, which are basically joke books, saying something on the cover like the benefits of going to college, then you open it and its blank or you can even reverse it and say the benefits of not going to college, and again, it is blank, but you need something on each page even if it's a number, also make it clear in your description and subtitle that this is a gag book. Some people don't even read the descriptions before they click 'buy now', then complain, so if it is on the subtitle page then there really are no excuses.

Scaling

I briefly touched on this earlier, but in order to succeed, you must scale your business or side hustle. This is simple really, if one book sells, keep an eye on it, if you sell above 4-5 a month, it is a pretty good niche and you should publish more books in this niche, but try different keywords and descriptions, this will take time but if there is proof of concept, don't ignore it as it could be a good selling niche. Another great way to scale is to take daily action, don't just sit on your hands. I will be totally honest, I'm not the type of person to sit around meditating all day, don't get me wrong, I do unwind in other ways, but I find it to be a waste of time and I could get a book done instead (don't take it personally, it's just how I work). Ultimately, this comes down to how much time you have and how hungry for success you are, now really is the time to act. The final way to scale is to run an ad, this again could not be simpler, just go to your book in your KDP back office and click 'promote and advertise', then follow the simple steps. Let Amazon do the heavy lifting here, if you have your keywords set up right, Amazon will do the rest more accurately. You will need to set a budget though. Make sure your book has sold before you run an advert as well, as this again shows proof of demand.

To scale your venture is to love your venture, and realistically, you should always be putting money back into your business when possible, this will always stand you in good stead and make your life easier. You can buy software, hire freelancers, run ads and get better technology, but reward yourself too. Most LCB businesses take at least a year to get any real results, that is on average, so don't give up, celebrate the little wins and focus on the solution and not the problem.

Resources

These are links to people who have helped me with my authoring journey, you will definitely get value out of these influencers:

Self-publishing with Dale on YouTube

Kelli publish on YouTube

Katherine Shelton on YouTube

Keith Wheeler books on YouTube

Conclusion

This concludes the course. I understand there is a lot to take on board here, especially as you may be new to this game. My aim was to produce an affordable education programme for beginners, so if you feel like you have gotten value out of my book, please consider leaving me a review on Amazon. As a side note, never pay for reviews of your notebooks/journals as that is against Amazon's terms and conditions. Thank you for taking the time to read through this book, I wish you all the best in your venture.